In Light, Always Light

New Women's Voices Series, No. 145

poems by

Angela Trudell Vasquez

Finishing Line Press
Georgetown, Kentucky

[handwritten: For Colleen Enjoy TXS! Love nyie]

In Light, Always Light

New Women's Voices Series, No. 145

"Poetry is the language of intensity. Because we are going
to die, an expression of intensity is justified."
C.D. Wright, *Cooling Time*

ACKNOWLEDGMENTS

I thank the editors of the following journals for accepting and publishing
these poems in print or online:

Cloudthroat—"Wheel Kids"
The Politics of Shelter—"Arboretum"
Raven Chronicles—"Chicago," "Woodstoves & Outhouses"
Return to the Gathering Place of the Waters—"In Light, Always Light," The
Photograph," & "Wild Prayer"
San Diego Poetry Annual 2015-2016—"Dark Knight"
Subtle Forces—"Patina," "Sea Burial"
Taos Journal of Poetry—"Fragments in Time"
Yellow Medicine Review—"Space Time," "What the Well Witnessed," &
"Winegardner Road"
Where I Want to Live—"Wheel Kids"
The Wisconsin Academy—"Scribbling," "Wheel Kids"
Wisconsin Democracy Campaign—"Dark Knight," "Synonymous"
Wisconsin Poet's Calendar (2019)—"Wheel Kids"
Woodland Pattern Book Center—"Space Time," "Wild Prayer"

Publisher: Leah Maines
Editor: Christen Kincaid
Cover Art: Devin P. Trudell
Author Photo: Nicole E. Taylor
Cover Design: Leah Huete

Printed in the USA on acid-free paper.
Order online: www.finishinglinepress.com
also available on amazon.com

Author inquiries and mail orders:
Finishing Line Press
P. O. Box 1626
Georgetown, Kentucky 40324
U. S. A.

Table of Contents

Wheel Kids

Chocolate children
race down the cul-de-sac
tight curls bounce
jeans t-shirts rise with air
clenched fists, taped bars,
tennis shoe brakes, no breaks
a shout   they cruise
out of sight of the window
bikes, scooters shake quake
skinny kid arms, legs, torsos
skin flattens—
neighbors straight arrows
shooting stars flesh flies
bodies grow wings.

Winegardner Road

We live on the last street
the river a sliver of bent willows
separates suburbs traces lost songs
downstream…

Fish hooks dangle, set deep in my heel.
Blood drips, smears the pavement scarlet.

We balance buckets of screws over door ways.
Small hands topple beams.
Trees cheer us on through plywood rectangles.
Saw dust clears nose, gushes tears.

I impale the meaty side of my palm on a nail
climbing the torn tree house.
I rip it up and off.

A skeleton farmhouse peals away
its planks. Wood dissolves.
Hidden walls, hallways mingle…

Tombstones sink into earth.
Fall back to sand, silt, slip under
fall oak leaves, red maple saplings.

The blood orange red sun sinks,
burns on the horizon
missing, gone ever since
like the newspaper boys
who disappeared the next summer.

Arboretum

Frames Mexican bones
bodies who built railroads
with broken backs, raw hands.

An 1880 census conceals us
carving holes in steel cars,
for light, night air, hanging
hammocks for sleeping wives
to rock under galaxies.

One woman rides the continent
follows her man from Zacatecas.
Thighs astride her clacking motorbike.
Belly swings on a swing sways on the rails until…

Where they lived in box cars until kids were grown.
Where postpartum was unknown
and unbalanced women got sent back.

Where my grandma, her cousins
hid on the school hill to eat quesadillas.

Neighbors claim the old man rode with Pancho Villa
when men in suits leap off skyscrapers in New York.

Where my mom and tia pretend not to speak English
teasing shopkeepers on the square.

Where my dad ran cross country to escape
those fences, farmland until he broke—
a mahogany streak on burnt clay tracks.

Where my uncle strove through bullets in Vietnam
dragging his buddy to the helicopter.

And grandmothers trade apples for pears
fingertips and ashy wrists
dig out change at the market,
dole out tortillas during meals.
One hand on the open flame,
one hand flutters holds the blue house dress.

Where peony roots divide on their own
sparking an arboretum of sweet pink light.
Whose perfume carries itself uptown
to the courthouse in drafts with garlic and chile.

Where my sister came   the day my grandfather was buried.
Water gushing graveside.

And summers meant volting between family houses.
Rhubarb sticks dipped in bone white sugar.
Rope swing thigh burns. Treasure hunts in the gully.

Where I visit now   water their parched Easter Lilies
        as they lie beneath the grass.

Thank them:

        for surviving Midwest winters, wars and lynchings,
        for firewood split, mole recipes on parchment,
        for raising people who love so much it hurts to swallow,
        for lessons on how small caramel women united overcome great
            sorrow,
        for sharing their one red lipstick and rose hand lotion when I
            was a girl flowering.

Woodstoves and Outhouses

Grandchildren fly on the rope swing
out back. She waits stirs the beans,
keeps the fire going.

What lies beneath her hands?

Wood smoke slips from a black belly stove,
red cinders fume from the night before.
Heat vibrates towards three boys in bed.
One raises his tousled head,
sees his Mom poke the embers
with an iron rod as tall as she is long.

What grows from her exhale?

Clean socks, shoes, pants—
three sets hang on wood pegs.
Quesadillas warm metal lunch pails.
Square shoulders trod to school.
Boys with no father but a mother,
old oak in high winds
with roots deep and green.

What apple bouquet greets her nose?

Open the world
to bumblebee tongue
breath of pollen, breathe.

What flavor rose?

Her sons go come back, go come back.
Greets them with her mulberry trees,
vermillion roses, thinning hair,
flowered house dresses, aprons.

Born at a Funeral

Caught, under the bed
baby dolls propped on pillows
stuffed animals against dark pink velour.
Her black curls bop, she reads
Cinderella to her "dollies"
in a voice husky from lack of use.
She lies on her stomach. Ankles twist.

> I spoke for her before she spoke
> for me when bus stop bullies lobbed spit ball bullets.
> Easy target: trumpet case, school books,
> extra credit books, glasses, braces, silent.

Little girl born at a funeral
when dirt clods hit the casket.
Her entry on a flood of salt tears, a family's
wails of grief. Fall ginger leaves scatter our names.

> When she began to open her mouth
> she wrote stories for her baby dolls.
> They rode horses, served tea, played
> mass using pickle slices for the host.

Her mother called her father
and began to weep over the wires
looping commas of sound
downtown to our house,
"She can talk. She can sing!"

Hamburger Gravy

Wrinkles line his face at eleven,
a sixth grade education saved
a hundred men on a Japanese island.
He knew how to ration outlast famine,
Iowa child of the depression.
No shirt, no shoes under his overalls,
wove newspapers for boots in winter.

Walked five miles a day,
a wolf dog mix companion,
mulberry tree staff.

One chocolate square per day
surrounded by enemies, he kept
his regime. Mind forever poisoned.
Sure it was "Them Japs" after
the Oklahoma City bombing;
but no, a boy, white, gun hungry—
a veteran who blew up preschool children
and glass to star dust. Human remains
floated over the city, sky sucked up
all those spirits into heaven, if you believe…
Grandpa made hamburger gravy, fried
potatoes, brewed beer, guzzled sweet
black coffee for hours telling stories.
Voice booms over the blond wood grain
once the color of his hair,
"I eat good…knew those chickens were bad,
farmer made them cannibals…Mary?"

California bound—
he rushed out of the bedroom,
when I visited.

Outlived all three of his wives,
My grandma's dresses doll clothes,
he said, watery blues smiling.
Her eyes at "The Fair," he bespoke
tractors, prize steers, pork
beauty queens, pumpkin eaters.
Saturday nights, before
she lost one leg then another,
standing on his massive feet,
they danced to honky-tonk music
and sang Glen Campbell's "Less of Me"
on the porch, she blind and twirling.

    Dandelion wine,
    striped overalls, six hands tall,
    voice gravel blue jeans.

Natchio

We drank Don Julio shots with the priest.
Gobbled fresh tortillas, pork mole, rice, beans.

Welcomed Natchio's seamstress mistress to the feast.
Paid the holy guide to rescue

Natchio's dead wife from damnation.
On our knees we chanted for a week.

A holy woman came to save her, light the way with words.
Rosary said at our place to free her from purgatory.

Bead by bead, fingertips tracing smooth cool pearl spheres,
circle to tail, lilt lift Spanish prayers.

Open house when Natchio's wife died.
I sat on his lap as a child read "The Family Circus."

Natchio scans the *Des Moines Register*. Smokes Lucky Strikes.
Carries perfume from last night.

Aftershave cover, obsidian glasses perch,
blood red eyes, whiffs of Jack Daniels.

What the Well Witnessed

And I choke on the conversation,
short black open flame marks tarnish copper pans,
nothing in the heavens prepared—
I was disgust boiling up myth root, I know why
she could not stand one more minute
in her in-law's cave sleeping in the corner
no way she would stick out that life
a beat wife,
a battered stump folded in two crying.
By Spring, she would leave—
because a water pitcher impaled her cheek
shattered her jaw. She would
get a divorce for 300 pesos, go back to her parents.
She stares into the bubbling beans: a boy, a girl,
it is the smell of their sun warm hair,
the way they clutched at her body feeding.
She grips the wooden spoon, cracks it in her hand,
a child with silk black hair to her waist enters the kitchen.
She lets the vision go—
calls her granddaughters *dolly*.
After all boys she has dollies of her own,
and the scent wave recedes a spell.
She grabs another spoon to stir the greens
adds a pinch of salt, garlic, hand flips a toasted tortilla
to the waiting plate on the Formica table, wipes her face clean.

Peony Springs—Newton, Iowa, Circa 1986

I.

White wood house on a large lot, vegetable garden out back—
chicken coops bee hives line pink cream peony plants.

Coral shrubs scatter the green—
      divided by a dead man's hands fifty years.

His flower heads droop with perfume and ants in spring.
      Herbaceous oasis blooms crimson up from the street.

II.

Cousins—
sneak a cold one
from the ice box.

We cruise past
    the dining room table
      wall of flesh
        the burn pit and raspberry bushes
          through the ravine to the seam
          the V peak of the hills
            where dappled light spills
              between rocks and discarded beer cans.

III.

We sit, share
sips and secrets:

      doors on the land
      who we want to kiss
      vortexes to the spirits
      where the long dead and buried
      come out to prop us up
      sit on the stairs, hold our hands,
      pat a sad back.

We feel them. Our stories unfold
at the kitchen table. We listen
to lore told by uncles and aunts.
People who die come back. Married
to place they leak downstairs, shake
their heads and sniff the beers.

      Say *yes, yes fight back.*

IV.

Back yard bowls fashion other worlds for us kinfolks—
      an emptiness where consciousness rings.

To see ancestors' ghosts   look twice   over your shoulder.

See caves of bones, hides worn, hand shaped tools, hidden
dreams awake asleep while walking
or on a hill
in lotus position
breathing wind transmissions
pollen, cotton seeds, fresh turned earth
blue jay wings, ripe nectarines.

V.

Trace fingers, outline words in the cool clear stream

      frogs croak, robins dip to drink,
      a raccoon halts   sees us
          pads soft into the gushing creek
              washes paws and face with back mitts
          bounces off with a nod.

We children of poor whites and migrants
say nothing
woods and wild animals common.

We walk back
hours have passed
      and still our people talk a steady stream.

Between the doors fifty bodies

      little ones in diapers
      dogs with sloppy tongues
      calico cats clean on the stairs.

          Line at the bathroom three cousins deep—
            television screen buried
              behind a sea of legs and blue jeans.

Space Time

I.

We are magic dying.

Pink peonies gasp tight ants assist open petals

no peony exists without ministrations of light

brick wall frames space between drive

a garden of red clay pots brightens balcony

all balconies lit with green light caress eyes

eyes mystery, upset images transform in skull

how we got here is fought over in courtrooms

people pretend to be god brandish fire sticks

hands tools, nails weapons

a newborn is a garden of purple heirloom potatoes

an angel reads minds from her high chair, babbles

mother feeds child smashed orange skin sweet potatoes with tiny spoon.

We are most vulnerable when we sit at the table with fork and knife.

II.

Early rose light calls from window

jack rabbits bound

flight occurs on ground.

Where are my crow friends?

Hawk brown circles school bathed in blue light

students descend stairs fade into brilliance

talks done talk begins

black pen scratches white paper

mind waxes   sheds peacock feathers.

How do you begin to think mired in thought and self-doubt?

Walk clears canvas, blank sheets beg

pull feet to mountain ascend.

Sea Burial

Backpacks, a week of groceries, no hospital
for 200 miles, no wheels, I survived—

on the island where once in a clearing
we came upon an animal meeting,
hooves and feathers flee, mass exodus.

There lies part of me, my man—
wedged beneath blinding white rocks.

Body whispers, blood and rot.

Until sediment slides down
the fifteen-foot cliff back to the sea.

Campfire ashes circle the base.

Where pelicans preen and eagles train
to feed, is our born too early zygote.

My two became one.

Female island ghosts told me
*sit in the water let life wash out and back
cool stone slabs your throne. We know.*

A sea burial. A hollow tree.
Limestone markers.

Wings Mimic Waves

Albatrosses guard the island, float on edges, wings mimic waves. They watch for intruders to these shores. Collective memory remains. Mayans shipped off to be slaves carved back to earth, stone. Jagged edges carry bones home, wash them up to sand, shore, rocks form new barrier reefs. Fish grow from marrow. Bones feed fish, people, the sea.

Pelicans defend the island from pirates, marauders. People lost in their hearts who seek to tame sky and land. Fools think they are stronger than the arcs that beat the shore: the heartbeat of the ocean, the Caribbean, the ceaseless stroke of green foam carving out its initials into sandstone, over and over.

Sentinels circle the island tilt black, glide on gusts, slide sideways follow shoreline, white bellies, necks, two tail feathers move independent, bide the wind. Mornings in Mexico, feathers punctuate sky, as far as eye can see, up and down the beach. Sea birds float sideways shadow the page, fly, as long as there are fish to eat.

The Photograph

Pelicans pose
on posts
at the pier,
highlight sun
going down,
point beaks,
preen for tourists
who snap shot
after shot.
Feather beasts
beat wings
against orange orb,
plunge head first,
in glass green waters
to fish, feed
at the cusp,
island coast.
Long beaks,
big downy breasts,
sideways way
of looking,
as if to say,
"I know you—
you want to look
like me,
all long nose
and Spanish
nobility."

What Sea Tentacles Did Not Tangle

The liberty bell clangs
wet tattered tots to wash ashore
on Lesbos island the foghorn bellows,
echoes wave passports.
Dark heads bob towards land, the volcano…

The sightless Parisian statue
peels back the clouds hovers her light
scans the water horizon for dank clothes,
flaying arms, denim legs
clinging to the rail, circles—
what sea tentacles did not tangle.

Clammy ice, cold threats
drag on women's teats, babies
cling to mothers' breasts,
life jacket hands hold in breaths.
Their chests inflate with sea air,
hold no liquid yet.

Civilians flee drone hits,
shoe soles slap pavement
bodies slam for cover dodge bricks, clay
splitting from their mortar past.
Store bought arms manufactured in the U.S.

Water welcomes when "world leaders"
condemn prayer rugs, hijabs
different names for the same beings
and not piles of gold or oil.

Blood floods psychic landscapes
stripped bones rattle sea beds.
Froth bodies swimming to shore
sing their names in the sand.

Synonymous

Woman wakes, wipes her face, stretches
walks two miles to mountain spring.

Gardener unwinds hose soaks palm tree roots
patrons sip coffee tea orange juice pinkies out.

At the top of the Alps
snow skips winter.

Salmon swims upstream hits dam, bleeds
no eggs will blossom this season.

Arroyos crack, dust spirals up and out, travels
bobcats coyotes rabbits hunt water.

Man in a jungle tilts black head drinks dew
from a banana leaf in the rose dappled morning.

Suburban well in Wisconsin leaches lead
seeks twenty-mile pipeline to drain Lake Michigan.

Back in hotel, guests request fresh towels
strawberries in winter, champagne baths.

Because

The dew spools in the far corner of the pasture,
a black and white Holstein dairy cow
licks her newborn calf clean.
Her pink tongue unfolding.
Emerald field grass stripes blink.
The calf looks over the hill
past barb wire fences, inter-
state traffic, rolling green
hills and faded white farmhouses,
across the north plains
towards the coral orb,
the heat of the rising sun
for the first time...

Sobs wrench my body cavity
for all in captivity. Tears
flood my shirt.
I pull over.

Let me sit in sadness for a spell.

I need to write this out.

> Died in her sleep.

> Her sister threw herself in front of a truck.

> Leaves behind three daughters.
> Her father called her, Negrita.
> The other two sisters were fair.

The mother
bathes her calf

mist rising
love, a pink tongue
in the morning
licks its forehead
dew blinks grass
fog lingers around their ankles
a vision
culled from the herd that crowds the hill.

Dark Knight

My husband of dark night and white meat
of close the drapes and turn off the lights,

my husband of ocean back and forehead continent
of bright sky eyes and cavern dimples

my man of sideways talking soft shoe
grooving liquid arms elbows waving

of basketball dreams and close calls
of farm fields for milking hay teats silos

of brooks that meander dogs that follow orders
of harvest the grain feed the cows water horses prairie streams

of peeled woods and sculpted weeds
of roads that cut and spill molasses

of prayers on barstools pews for others
of deer hunting and butchering bother

of take the land wrestled from another
of planned extermination and cleansing

of beat the child spoil the mother
the woman the house enslave the men,

of sorry we are doing it again,
this is inherited grief—blood on concrete.

Patina

Body scars older lives tongues caresses
whip marks spilled milk broken fences:
my skin is a patina of conquerors, the conquered,
slave smiles, earth hands flattened
by the press of burnt tin, wheelbarrows.

Sleek hair shows up white
now and then when thoughts of carnage
and lost people slay pigment.

Survivors can live through lines
on a page. Their voices ringing in pencil,
in ink. Beyond death, art speaks.

I have always been a woman.
Your sisters' blood lines pulse fire in your veins.
Our wee ventricles burst on occasion.

Brain beats still asleep muses on all
the people you know who have passed
to the grave, to vases of bone and ash—
who walk in dreams. Speak lines
of poetry in the dark.

Their voices alive at night.

Homework

Where postcards, posters from Paris, London, Mexico,
lithographs from the past, old prints picked up in travels, hang
out with "cannot read books" in Spanish on bookshelves.

Where ancestors hold places of worship in the old family oak hutch
smile back at me from the 40s, 50s saying, *"yes you have done much*
but not without our help and not so much, mija."

Where deck chairs sit, long for bones
in between snow storms, drenching rains,
clothes piercing winds, where hawks, woodpeckers,
bald eagles flit, and crows talk big
outside our bedroom windows call us to wake,
open the shades, greet the day with sun
salutations, black coffee, honey
with buttered toast, green tea.

Where hard pressed beneath the sheets I swim
in: "to do" sleep, "forbidden love" sleep,
"big fear of falling" sleep. Sleep, wash me
clean. Reboot my brain. Spine snaps back.
Cats stir. Husband gone most days. Travel dreams
carry me until I wake in my own time, year, day, bedroom...

Where pictures look back at me at 20, 30 and 40
where faded curls from the 80s are pressed
between clear pages before you found me   Mexican me,
where dear man lies on a sofa,
cats book ending his head and feet—
devouring texts not checked out in centuries.

Where red Burgundy sits after a icy commute
and poems sprout wings from dead trees,
sink under skin, seep flow from bloody fingertips
and fly out into the world on their own velocity.

Sound Scape

Plane engines whir
leaves clap
footsteps crush
red earth crunch
dry twigs laugh
tiny bird chirps
gecko scramble
water splashes
hand carved rows
corn bathing grows
fan whirs behind
sidewalk voices float
disembodied hello—
lands near,
bees buzz cackle
wings hover
fly wings trickle
water soaks
red earth drinks
whippoorwill calls
motorcycles buzz
writer cries out
road runner scratches
tree leaf quakes
cool breeze blows
hair joins chorus
wind whistles ears -
farmer kneels, knee
hits ground
plants leap
crab apples drop
red earth receives
ants march to feed.

Coneflowers

Wildflowers lift the interstates flood me
    with amethyst, aqua, crimson, amber,
        dying emerald leaves and golden forests.

I inhale red maples flashing. Feel the crunch
    and squish beneath the tires. The roots
        crack seams beaten by semi wheels
            in forty below and a blue coneflower pulses
                next to a crane harvesting the shoulder.

The Train Cuts the Prairie in Two

Makeupless I ride with coffee and dead poets. I put on lipstick at first light, rearrange my papers. Who am I writing for? Cars roll by small town country kids' graffiti. Rural children color bridges just like in big cities. Do they dream of escape: a NBA career or being a CPA? How to avoid parenting? Moving to the city? Who lived on these prairies before railroads breathed coal? What rough hands laid track, raised the pickaxe, cleared fields, dug trcnches, signed evacuation orders? An unshaven man across from me drinks a tall boy. It is not quite noon. He falls asleep. Three Budweiser cans slip, roll between his laced boots. His body hugs his pack. Union Pacific, what backs built you? Who lived on your plank shores, slept in your box cars? Hoboes, families of four, railroad worker families who carved windows and hung hammocks to sleep as they rolled under the stars? Or children who grew up to travel to foreign countries where high speed bullet trains never stop moving? Where you can drink champagne on some veranda overlooking water? Any body of water will do in a parched parcel. This is cruel eat gruel land. People ask for money at highway intersections, scramble for coins when lights change. Icy winds saunter, shake the windows, blow the sleeping man's hair from its skull base. His shirt ruffles. His duffel bag seeps socks, magazines. The bag may implode in his grip. Cats look out from sliding glass windows. When we stop for more passengers, the felines make eye contact with the metal beasts, stare into the windows.

Binaries

One. Niece colors at barn door table, smiles looks at her brother drawing Batman & Robin, good guys, bad guys. She smiles to say, "look at me, look at us, I am coloring." Black curls, size of frozen juice cans, jostle when her chubby arms scribble red and yellow. Her brother calls her Chuck. Her real name is Raven. My youngest sister's daughter. Before she was born her dad dreamed her tall with good hair. Strands more Mexican than Puerto Rican, straight and fine, black silk, her mother's long tresses. My nephew's hair shows his African roots like his father's. Henry and Raven. Hank and Chuck. Green eyes jewel both their faces. We dine at Café Con Leche. People who could be distant cousins scurry bring pancakes, eggs, bacon, coffee and sweets. We hear the origins of Chuck. Batman shrank Robin to save the day, called him his little Chucka Mucka before he made him normal size. Justice prevailed in less than a half hour. My nephew loves Bears to Packers, Bulls to Bucks, policemen and firemen who save the day. Once on the playground he shared on the monkey bars he wanted to be a policeman. I said we can talk about that later. He said, "Grandma does not like them either." He knows. He is six. Binary columns work for his brain right now. I think about his light afro how many men with his hair texture spend birthdays behind bars, rot in holes, shake hands with the death penalty, swung from trees like "Strange Fruit" for entertainment. He will know this later. I push him on the swing. Instruct him to go higher. "Pump your legs, keep your knees pressed together, lean back, use your core strength to the moon and back!" Playground people stare and chuckle. I watch him finish color Batman and Robin across the table black and blue crayons melt in his caramel hands.

Scribbling

I prefer crowds with voices echoing
up and down the train cars, city bus gears singing   *stop here*
exhaust spewing, laughs rolling to the page—
boots, heels, sneakers step on and off the curb,

      voices flood ears become stolen dialogue in ink.

I write in public to feel stilettos slap pavement,
for the roar of pigeons in flight, the scent of yeast
to count those who stop to give the cold and knocked about
coins on the corner. Watch a little boy with his grandma
hand out raisins, buy their newspapers, deliver popcorn
balls, candy canes, cards full of glitter, signed
in a seven-year-old scrawl   *God Bless You.*

I write so we can rest our bones,
our driving force to live without capture,
to forget about death float words
to the page without waking rise above
ego brain   scribbler with no name
observe life teeming: chipmunks who skedaddle
at the crow's shadow, squirrel highways in city parks, on power lines, pitches
to see young men assist a tottering woman
and her bags cross the street when traffic does not
stop for thin bones, the way *el sol*
goes to sleep, casts a halo over structures humans
construct to shield people from ice sheets whistling
across lakes, prairies, the summer rays that burn
foreheads and cheeks stamping a fury

      so we can sleep at night embrace the soft dark light.

Chicago
(for Eschikagou)

Metal sides rise to sky
on banks of water so blue
it hurts eyes.

This water, holy water takes lives,
ships lie at bottom
rice paddies forgotten.

City named after wild onion
now brick, mortar, steel and glass
planted in underpass survive.

Lake slides from river, river
reversed eases merchants,
men don black suits.

Who changes the flow but man?
Ghost river blows hats, winds steal land,
bone people shiver in winter breath.

Wild Prayer

Brown earth floors
breathe feet, sweaty bodies

we glow, glisten, meet
leaping in midflight,

the swivel in the mirror
we are magic dying

blooming in our bodies
bare soles touch dead trees

arms raise carry twist
praise all that sings

praise goddess monkey teacher
from up north who left

to dance on haloed ground
on the edge of blue sky lakes
with sisters round and round.

In Light, Always Light

Grass strands gleam weave, undulate from the window

The vendor screams *build the wall*
lifts his hands works the crowd
looks at me   sells more t-shirts.

My mind waxes. Brilliant wet glass winks, waves shine back
        my reflection.

I am dazzled by the sun glinting off my cat's whiskers. He lays
on his back, flanks splayed by the deck   half-shade, half-light.

First graders play football on marigold carpet in our shared back yard.
The smile on their faces when they catch it warms us—
childless apartment dwellers behind glass walls.

The poet reads a book of poems then walks to the park to think.
She does not know what she is going to do   hike
the sled hill or swing on the swing. If no children are present
she will swing until her stomach says no, then descend
from her height among the tree tops and head home.
She circles the preserve full of earth thoughts: falling leaf
music, crashing, crushing sounds and auburn smells
float up from her footsteps.

She thinks.

We spin on Earth's axis   half-blinks of history.

Fragments in Time

Moonlight radiates down
children do not mourn
parents buy new shoes
       rabbits copulate in grass
           leap over each other and dash.

Cracking open a woman a child births itself.

Bodies arch over steering wheel
fog condenses glass.
We find each other... *a voice in my head says he is the one.*

After the fall people see
       they are not   who they thought.
Fortify hope in a wooden barrel
send her over water to live
in her grandparents' stable.
Wait out the peril: dust storms,
trains tracks pounding down her back,
nails piercing flesh, hand rotting still attached.

Shoulder length hair, khaki crescendo,
camel jacket wind sails, ghost bodies
hang around invisible ankles, graze cement.
He follows me, shouts from corners   *beware, beware.*

Grandson places hand in sandpaper fold,
parachutes to shoulders, peers down fields
where white herons alight, flocks migrate
nest at feet of skyscrapers, exhaust fumes,   birch oasis.

Moon beams flood evening, babies born with wings
flee fire steeples, plant pine forest temples
along the shores of ancient rivers. Start over.

What was our first language?

Poets resist death of a people
fingertips bless pen, paper.
Full moon halo crowns campus   new humans born   two hearts beating.

Sound.

Angie Trudell Vasquez received her MFA in creative writing with a concentration in poetry from the Institute of American Indian Arts in Santa Fe, New Mexico. Her work has been published in *Taos Journal of Poetry, Yellow Medicine Review, Raven Chronicles, Return to the Gathering Place of the Waters,* and *Cloudthroat* among other journals and anthologies. She has a page and poems from her first two books on the Poetry Foundation's website, and was a Ruth Lilly fellow as an undergraduate at Drake University. She has new work forthcoming from *RED INK: International Journal of Indigenous Literature, Arts & Humanities.*